MAKING
THE MOST OF
BEDROOMS

MAKING
THE MOST OF
BEDROOMS

KAREN HOWES

RIZZOLI
NEW YORK

For Pooks

First published in the United States of America in 1997 by
RIZZOLI INTERNATIONAL PUBLICATIONS, INC.
300 Park Avenue South, New York, NY 10010

First published in the United Kingdom in 1997 by
Conran Octopus Limited
37 Shelton Street
London WC2H 9HN

ISBN 0-8478-2016-5
LC 96-71509

Commissioning Editor   Denny Hemming
Project Editor   Sarah Sears
Art Editor   Ruth Prentice
Picture Research   Clare Limpus
Production   Jill Beed
Illustrator   Sarah John
Editorial Assistant   Paula Hardy

Printed in Hong Kong

CONTENTS

BASIC PRINCIPLES

The four walls of your bedroom surround a very private world; its style, colour and contents will be stamped with your personal touch. The role played by a bedroom will vary, however, and to define the requirements of these different roles should be your first consideration when you are planning from scratch. Nevertheless, if you carefully assess the available space and follow some basic rules, it should be both easy and enjoyable to create the perfect bedroom sanctuary.

PLANNING

The flexibility of today's lifestyle and the wide variety of environments which we choose to call 'home' ensure that more than a degree of thought has to go into deciding on the location of the bedroom.

Traditionally, in a house, bedrooms are located upstairs and near a bathroom, separated at a discreet distance from those rooms – living room, dining room or kitchen – in which you entertain. So for those with the means to have a whole house at their disposal, there is generally less scope for originality because the bedrooms will have been planned as part of the fabric of the building. For the majority of city dwellers, living in apartments, basements, houseboats, converted lofts, schools and even converted warehouses, choosing the location of the bedroom can be a more personal and original decision.

Most people have already decided which room will be where before they purchase or move into a new property, their decisions governed – or at least influenced – by the dimensions of the available rooms. The living room nearly always acquires the only available fireplace and the largest floor area. But it does not have to be like this.

Take the time to sit down right at the beginning, over a large mug of tea, and analyse your lifestyle and your requirements. Do you entertain a lot? How much time are you likely to spend in your bedroom? Will you use it for anything other than sleeping? How much time do you actually spend awake at home? The list can be endless!

Depending on how honest you are, your bedroom could easily, and should perhaps, occupy the largest room you have available; leave your friends to sit on top of one another in a kitchen-cum-living room instead. If you live in a *pied-à-terre* or studio you will inevitably entertain in your bedroom, as it will be the only room. You could easily apply the same principle in a loft conversion or a barn, however. In all these cases, one large room can prove to be remarkably adaptable. You can designate one end as 'the bedroom', and hide the bed behind a screen, raise it on a gallery, or disguise it during the daytime as a large cupboard (closet), whether it be upturned and stored inside or perched like an eyrie on the top.

On the other hand, why not make a focal point of the bed? Why disguise it? Do this deliberately, however, rather than by mistake, for it can be very expensive to buy a bed that becomes a white elephant. And it is all too easy to make mistakes amidst the excitement and enthusiasm that always surrounds a new home. Buy the bed to fit the room, or you may suffer the consequences: one of my friends fell in love with a substantial four-poster, which became the talking point of the village because it had to reside in all its glory in the centre of his living room. No other room in the cottage was able to accommodate its girth and weight.

A bedroom that has a permanent status as a bedroom gives you great scope. First of all, bearing in mind reference points such as windows and doors, built-in cupboards (closets) and existing lighting sockets, as well as specific items of furniture that you cannot live without, decide on the best location for the bed. What sort of bed do you see yourself in? Are you intending to fill up your room with lots of furniture? If you have the space, what about a separate dressing room, or storage room, for shelves and additional

A PLATFORM PERFORMANCE

Platforms are an increasingly fashionable solution to the dilemma of finding a suitable bed. In this Japanese-style studio, architect Nico Rensch has successfully incorporated a central clothes storage unit into the platform, which acts as a headboard and as a base for flexible lighting, as well as providing hanging space. Built-in drawers make an architectural feature of the back wall and flank a minimalist blue glass washbasin. The shower is a glassed-in cubicle in the far corner of the room.

An emphasis on light wood in this airy, clapboard bedroom (previous page, left) unites walls, ceiling and floor with an interesting, if mannered, use of horizontal and vertical planking. A simple, painted, wooden bed, its crisp blue and white cushions and bed cover echoed by other cushions on the window seat, completes the fresh look, while rush matting adds to the overall natural feel.

Orderliness does not have to be crisp and empty. This storage unit for the clothes-conscious male (previous page, right) illustrates that it can be idiosyncratic too.

PLANNING

- Decide on a style for your bedroom and stick to it. Don't compromise.
- If your bedroom is 'on show', drape an interesting cover over the bed and scatter it with cushions to transform it into a day bed. Store your bedclothes in an old-fashioned blanket box or wicker basket at the end of the bed, in specially designed drawers under the bed, or in a cupboard (closet) – wherever space permits.
- Establish what furniture has to be accommodated in addition to the bed before you choose potentially too small a room. Then choose a bed that suits the shape of bedroom.
- Do not allow the guest bedroom to degenerate into a junk room. Have ample drawer and cupboard (closet) space or store junk in such a way that becomes a decorative feature.
- Allow the limitations of the space to dictate the terms in awkwardly shaped rooms. If an attic, design a few shelves or cupboards to fit the irregular wall pattern if traditional furniture is inappropriate.
- Do not economize on lighting. Explore the various systems available until you find an effect that is right for you.

■ 9

hanging space, leaving the bedroom free for the more unusual paraphernalia of your life? If you are sharing a house with friends, incorporating some sort of sitting room into the bedroom might be useful, in order to give you a little additional privacy and to avoid having to watch television endlessly from the bed.

Guest bedrooms tend to be the smallest rooms in the house. The size of bed is therefore very important. If this room does not have to perform a dual role, functioning as part-time study, work room or dumping ground when not inhabited by guests, you should give as much thought to its layout as a bedroom as you would to your own. Guests like

to feel that you have taken some trouble. A pretty chair beside a small table that can double as dressing table and desk, some interesting pictures, a few strategically chosen books by the bed, ambient light and flowers for a personal touch go a long way to making guests feel welcome.

En-suite bathing

Incorporating a bath into your bedroom will require considerable thought. Although the romantic appeal of being able to roll out of bed straight into a hot bath, or vice versa, carries great sway, the practical problems created by lack of privacy, general plumbing installation, and the

OPEN SPACES

A master bedroom should know the luxury of space. The location of the bed is important if the room is not as large as this one (far left) and built-in cupboards (closets) can contribute. If two rooms are opened up into one, the resulting skeleton support can become a feature of the much-enlarged new look, and you can incorporate a cosy sitting area, too. If the bedroom is at the top of the house, why not enlarge your space still further by building upwards: you could have an eyrie up in the roof space, only accessible via a ladder.

Guest bedrooms (left) tend to occupy smaller rooms, often devoid of interesting features. Just because these rooms are only used irregularly, however, it does not mean that you cannot liberate your imagination in them. Some tend to double up as a dumping room, so make sure your junk is constantly hidden from the surprise guest – here concealed under a table draped in fabric which serves as a headboard. While wardrobes (closets) are really unnecessary for the temporary visitor and take up valuable space, ensure that there is a chair for their suitcase and a couple of hooks with coat hangers on the back of the door.

■ 11

effects of steam and condensation must be considered, especially in cold climates. Where space is at a premium – in guest rooms, for instance – you might be able to plumb in a small handbasin or modern shower unit in one corner to give you a little additional privacy. Those of you with a romantic inclination, but without the means, could always introduce an antique water pitcher and basin, either for purely decorative purposes or, as it was originally intended, as a functioning, portable washbasin.

BATHROOMS LAID BARE

Accommodating bathrooms in small living spaces – especially for guests – can prove expensive on space as well as posing nightmarish plumbing problems. One alternative is to place the bathtub in the bedroom itself. To have your bath as close to the bed as it is in this converted and modernized attic room (left) can be very convenient for the indolent, but the tiled floor and general austerity of the room are especially suited to a warm climate. Practical problems such as steam and condensation perhaps account for the absence of curtains, carpets and bed hangings.

An alternative scheme might be to conceal a handbasin and storage shelves behind the headboard of the bed (far left). The bath, located against the far wall, is open along the side but screened at either end for a little privacy, creating an environment that is conducive to long, luxurious soaks. This layout will also go some way in reducing the problems of condensation in the bedroom, especially if an extractor fan is also installed. As a means of saving space, this arrangement provides a very workable solution while the design clearly defines the room into two areas.

SPACE EXPLOITATION

Guest bed, your own bed or comfortable den – in any case, this half landing under the eaves displays not only an aesthetic but an ingenious use of space. Again, the platform bed has been employed, though here it is a little impractical as far as making the bed is concerned – and access might be rather inelegant, too. But it does leave the bed at the right level for the clever cupboard (closet) units, and the proportions of the room, governed by the low ceiling height, work well in relation to it. As an alternative to the oil painting which is used here as a headboard, you could paint an imaginative bedhead on the wall or hang up an interesting and colourful piece of fabric. As a multi-purpose area, this bedroom combines as study and library. To create a really cosy and inviting lounger for reading, the bed could be loaded with comfortable cushions in muted, but co-ordinated colourways. The choice of pale wood for the shelving and cupboard doors, the uncluttered surfaces and the white-painted floorboards all combine to enhance the light atmosphere in this roof conversion.

Dual-purpose space

Multi-purpose rooms require discipline, particularly at the planning stage. If your bedroom is to double as another room on a permanent basis, it is important to establish a balance between the two intended functions at the very beginning. If you envisage sleeping in your library/study, your wall space will probably be taken up in housing your collection of books. Where will you put your clothes, shoes, hats, handbags and the clutter that tends to accumulate in the bedroom? Free-standing storage units may prove useful in this context. Choose bedside tables with drawers, boxes and plastic storage containers which can slip under the bed; perhaps you can leave one wall free for a wardrobe (closet). If you need a writing surface in the room, take over some of the drawers of a desk for clothes storage. An additional wall could be saved if you designed one of the bookshelves to fit around the bedhead, and building lights into the shelving saves space, too. If you have a television, position it at a good height in one of the bookshelves opposite the bed, and then find a similar home for your stereo, remembering that you will want frequent access – stylish and practical space-saving.

BARE ESSENTIALS

Modern can often mean minimal and this bedroom is no exception, located on a landing of a very slender house and benefiting from the light from numerous narrow windows. Minimal also means 'no clutter' and even in a room designed to serve several purposes, there is a distinctly economic use of furniture. The table or working surface collapses neatly against the central partition of the room, leaving a single chair and side table. Discreetly concealed behind this partition and accessible by the short set of stairs, is a bathroom, luxuriating in the sunlight. There are no paintings to break up the architect's clean lines. Instead, texture provides the decoration by way of rattan, metal and polished wood. It is a clever manipulation of a small and awkward space.

One-room living

One room or studio living – the way many of us live in large cities – is generally a euphemism for personal chaos! An environment in which you combine living, working, playing and sleeping is often achieved with minimal expense but with maximum stress levels. There is no greater challenge than condensing your belongings to fit your current living space. What to take and what to leave behind – and where? Attics and storage rooms of long-suffering friends and relations suddenly mushroom with dustbin bags containing valuable chunks of your life, yet the conundrum of how to accommodate the items you insist on keeping with you can produce ingenious storage ideas.

The motto for living in one room has to be 'Keep it simple'. It must be applied to the style of furniture, the decoration of the room, the objects and personal clutter. It is important to maintain a sense of space, particularly if the room is a modern unit and has a clean and streamlined look. Remember that the way you light the space is equally important and can make a boring room much more atmospheric – you can use low pools of light rather than overhead blanket lighting, candles for softness, or even small uplighters in the corners of the room.

If you are to live in a room that does not belong to you, studio rooms in old Victorian terraces, with their high ceilings and bow-fronted windows, accommodate more readily the personal touches you bring with you; living in a modern space requires a knack. Swathes of fabric can transform the grimmest room, helping to disguise ghastly wallpaper and less-than-perfect furnishings and cocooning you in a cosy refuge from the outside world, without causing undue damage to walls or ceiling.

Studio land is often a temporary waiting room, a short-term answer to that endless search for accommodation in an overcrowded city, or perhaps a *pied à terre* for occasional use. Studios can actually be purpose-built, so you can condense your life into one room with style. It helps if you are naturally tidy and own only a few possessions, lack of storage space creating another whole host of problems for those encumbered with a life's worth of goods and chattels. Studio units in modern blocks provide a basic space which you can adapt to suit your lifestyle. The secret is to choose your furniture carefully: a day bed that converts easily into a comfortable bed at night; a modular table and chairs for eating, working and other purposes; and accessories that add to the impression of spaciousness. To this end, opt for blinds rather than curtains, which take up valuable space. Use a screen, just to add another dimension to your four walls. And you can use a sliding door or wall panel to separate the bath and kitchen areas from the main room.

Awkward and unorthodox spaces

Imagination and patience are required in equally large quantities when you are planning a bedroom in an awkward space – and any room that is not square is awkward. Variable wall and ceiling heights can pose problems too, when the eaves of a roof come right down to floor level; effectively where there is no 'room' at all but where an area has to be created. Following the one-room-living principle, the simple approach is normally the most successful. Adventurous ideas can lead, if you decide to cope by yourself, to disastrous consequences. It is essential to seek professional advice if you are thinking about an attic conversion and any other building work that requires a knowledge of structural engineering.

It is fun to sleep in unorthodox areas, however, so creating a platform for a mattress where before there was no space for a bed at all, can be extremely satisfying. If you hoard clothes and possessions to the point where nothing else will fit into your designated bedroom, build a strong platform above your wardrobe (closet) and sleep up there! If the room is tiny, create a platform under the window. Be adaptable and you cannot fail.

As everyone is obsessed with utilizing space, rooms take shape in the most unlikely locations (below left). Place a mattress on an extended window seat, use the deep cupboards beneath to store the duvet and any additional pillows, and you have created a bedroom out of nothing, lit by natural light and one small reading lamp. And although it has essentially evolved out of practical constraints, this bedroom is characterized by compactness and originality, making it nestlike and cosy.

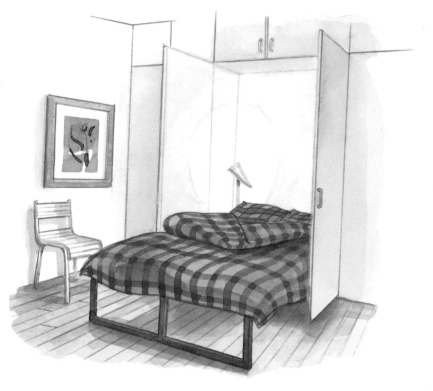

UP AND AWAY

Dealing with awkward spaces is always a challenge and trying to accommodate beds will magnify the difficulty as their length and weight create obvious problems. One way of sidestepping this problem (opposite, right) is to put the bed in a cupboard (closet). Built of light aluminium, with neat folding legs, these beds can be literally folded into a specially designed cupboard (closet) and shut away, together with slim duvet and pillows – a great way to avoid that daily chore of making the bed. The space they vacate can then be occupied by a table and chairs, and the room given a totally different function.

Lofts provide additional space but often in a very restricted form. The angle of the roof can be so acute that the only place a bed will fit is right in the middle of the room, where there is barely sufficient space for any other furniture. In this example (left) dormer windows not only shed more light, but also mean two single beds can be situated neatly side by side under the eaves.

■ 19

Storage

Few of us are naturally tidy-minded and a tidy bedroom seems to be one of life's more unattainable aspirations, but do try not to design a bedroom environment that is completely inappropriate to your lifestyle. If your clothes tend to lie around in heaps for days, the minimalist bedroom is not for you. You need rows of cupboards (closets) and bottomless drawers. Invest in a few high-sided storage boxes to contain the debris that normally ends up under the bed, or buy a bed with built-in drawers – ideal for packing away the duvet. If short of space, be economical with non-functional furniture. It is very easy to transform an old school trunk, by covering it with a kelim or old rug, to provide additional storage space at the foot of the bed and a surface for books and magazines – and it is far more space-effective than a mere bench.

Storage can be decorative as well as functional. Doors can be imaginatively painted or stencilled, or clad in fabric to match the bed linen or bed hangings. Cheaper alternatives include using coloured paper, or creating collages of postcards and memorabilia. You could remove the doors completely and replace them with rattan blinds. There are lots of ways to bring a cupboard (closet) to life.

Storage units can also become a structural feature of the bedroom. If space is short, you could place your mattress on top of free-standing storage units and make a

Storage at its most basic, yet most effective, is illustrated in this small understated bedroom (left) in which industrial metal shelving units have been erected along one wall, the only concession to decoration being the extravagant wrought-iron bedstead and the lengths of bright red fabric used as rudimentary blinds. Hat stand, basket-weave tray and a universal drawer unit provide a plethora of storage possibilities (above), while a more organized and stylized approach to storage has been taken in the bedroom (right). The basic divisions have been achieved using single rows of bricks, painted white, while the various compartments have been alternately curtained-off or fitted with simple plank doors.

BEDROOM STORAGE

- Try and combine more than one function in any one storage element. Wall-to-wall fitted cupboards (closets) could include mirror doors or incorporate a washbasin and, in addition to hanging space, provide storage for all those cumbersome bags and suitcases which always end up under the bed.

- If averse to mirrors, use glass-fronted cupboards (closets) and display your clothes. As a focus of the bedroom, the cupboards (closets) will provide additional depth to the room and can be discreetly lit. Serried ranks of underwear, shirts, etc., interspersed with books and objects and even the occasional picture, will turn your storage into a conversation piece.

- Open shelving can take care of those problem areas under the stairs and eaves but can gather dust and leave clothes less than pristine. Simple curtains or individual storage boxes can be used to protect delicate items.

- Storage units can also be used as room dividers; clothing rails in bedroom corners can be hidden behind screens covered in either fabric or paper.

self-styled sleeping platform. If aerial suspension does not appeal to you, use the units as room dividers – either as a series of screens or around the bed to create some privacy.

Lighting

The importance of lighting in a room cannot be over-emphasized. Strategically placed lamps can transform the most unimaginative room. Retailers have finally recognized the need for sophisticated and appropriate lighting, and there is something to suit everyone's requirements. You can choose from a great variety of standard bases, high-tech flexible stems, spots, uplighters and downlighters. Experimenting with lighting is not cheap, however, so it is probably better to start by looking at some basic principles alongside what you already have.

Forget overhead light: it will kill any atmosphere – particularly important in the bedroom. If you have always used standard bedside lamps but find that they are too harshly bright in their new environment, use bulbs of a lower wattage. Experiment with different shades; drape dark-coloured fabric over the existing shade to test a tone; have your lights on a dimmer switch so that you can adjust them to suit your immediate requirements; *in extremis*, place the lamp base on the floor to act as an uplighter.

Candles are cheap and will guarantee atmosphere. Metal-backed wall sconces reflect the candle light and so increase illumination in the room generally, but silver foil will achieve the same effect. You must remember to consider all aspects of bedroom life in your lighting plan: vanity units and dressing tables will need brighter, more directional lighting, and equally vital is the positioning and efficiency of reading lights.

SWITCHED ON

Lighting can make or mar the overall effect of a bedroom. Your first consideration should be practical for there is nothing more irritating than trying to read in bed with inadequate light, or having the shadow of your head thrown onto the page because of a badly placed lamp. However, the exciting variety of lighting available in the shops means that boring old bedside lamps on tables can be a thing of the past.

This light, white bedroom (far left) admits natural light through internal glass bricks. The choice of artificial light creates an interesting architectural focus. The lamps, on flexible arms, can be turned down for reading or turned away to reflect against the wall for a more muted, atmospheric effect.

Similarly, this plain white room (left) with decorative headboard and matching bed cover, has been transformed by the sculptural style of the lighting scheme. Positioned at each corner of the bed, the standard lamps are sufficiently tall to throw light on the bed as well as around the room, with two shelves positioned within the metal structure for necessities – an alarm clock, for example, and even a book or two.

STYLE

Style is a personal attribute which
requires neither extraordinary wealth
nor valuable possessions; if you have
style, you will be able to create
an environment in which you can live in
harmony with your surroundings. For you
will understand, and be able to
interpret, what works for you and your
day-to-day existence. The elusiveness of
style creates gurus out of interior
designers, and yet style is really only a
subjective synonym for good taste –
'You've either got it, or you haven't.'

COUNTRY

It is all too easy to be patronizing in interpreting what is meant by 'country style'; the concept as it is defined by magazines and marketing today is romanticized and often insulting to the rural world. Just as country themes tend not to work in the city, big city ideas for a humble country cottage can prove equally out of context.

Every property must be allowed to retain its individual atmosphere, even in the search for that elusive country idyll. After all, what undoubtedly attracted you to living in the country in the first place was the house or cottage and its location; its isolation, perhaps; the scope it has for a wonderful garden; the sense of getting back to nature. We all tend to over-romanticize our need for fresh air and wide open spaces, yet within that heightened sensitivity lies the true interpretation of our innate sense of country style.

The bedroom is naturally the most susceptible to the country influence, since here you can create an atmosphere of rustic tranquillity to suit your own interpretation. Often cosy in proportion and with small, low windows, cottage bedrooms tend to be dominated by the bed, leaving little room for other furniture. If this is a weekend retreat, then seasonal influences must play their part in the style of the bedroom. Muslin curtains, or no curtains at all over small windows, would allow summer's early light to filter gently into the bedroom. Heavier duty curtains could be substituted for those cold winter nights and sluggish, wet country mornings, when your inclination is to snuggle deeper under the colourful quilts and layers of thick blankets that transform country beds into nests for hibernating humans.

The city bedroom's country cousin can happily adopt an eclectic look: odd pieces of furniture from local antique shops, with no obvious function but fantastic form. Objects and well-worn textiles can also contribute to the rustic charm of a country bedroom. Rooms are usually smaller, so less furniture is required, with less emphasis on the finish of uneven walls and scrubbed floorboards. Armchairs should embrace you like old friends, tables and cupboards (closets) should be softened and rounded with age, beds should creak at your approach, linen sheets and quaint quilts redolent with the scent of freshly picked lavender should flow over the bed, with a pitcher of clover and meadow flowers on a neighbouring table. Each detail is important in setting the scene, creating a very special atmosphere that you can metaphorically bottle and carry with you.

RURAL RETREATS

These two images typify country style. Both rooms are small and have low ceilings, the bed in each case occupying most of the available space. Simple beds can be made cosy and inviting by combining colourful cotton quilts with a variety of pillows in similar tones, or by hanging a simple calico curtain around the bedhead to soften the austere effect of a wrought-iron bed.

Style in the bedroom can be as simple as an imaginative detail of a headboard (previous page, left). Located in a room with walls painted a glowing colour, the room needs no other visual adornments. Old printing-block storage units have been positioned on the wall between two barley twist posts, topped with a golden setting sun. The arrangement of pillows in a variety of stripes is a cheap and jolly way to liven up the bed, creating an eye-catching effect.

Counterbalancing this image is a detail of crisp lace on the turndown of a sheet and a lovely, dainty bolster cover, tied with pale blue ribbon (previous page, right). Antique sheets and lace pillowcases make a romantic addition to any bed.

HELPFUL HINTS

- Have the courage of your convictions. If you lack confidence in your own sense of style, you can glean a lot from the myriad books and magazines available on the subject. Remember, though, that every style has its place.
- Be daring in your use of colour and fabric. Combine different elements to create a new and exciting effect. If something does go wrong, you can always rectify it.
- Be inventive with your furniture. Practically no item has to be used solely for the purpose for which it was originally intended.
- Never turn up your nose if friends or relatives offer you a chance to hunt for treasure when they are cleaning out their attics. Amazing results can be achieved from unlikely beginnings: priceless antiques have been found at rummage sales, after all!
- Experiment with different looks until you find the one that feels right for you. This can often take several attempts, so do not get depressed.
- If in doubt, choose one strong element – a piece of furniture, a rug or a length of fabric – and let your design develop around it.

SHABBY CHIC

You do not necessarily have to have lots of money to create a shabby chic bedroom. However, you do need plenty of self assurance if you are going to combine successfully a selection of apparently incongruous elements in the same room. While magazines might suggest that anything goes in shabby chic, what separates the sheep from the wolves is one person's ability to see which faded fabric will work with which piece of distressed furniture, and which ancient mirror would add the appropriate sense of faded grandeur without looking self-conscious. Do not try too hard or you may find that you have created a disastrously unkempt effect instead. To produce the look that makes old and worn look rich and welcoming, you need a good eye for design – and enough historical knowledge to ensure that you use styles that are sympathetic to each other.

It may be the acquisition of an antique mirror, or a vast wardrobe (closet), or even some chintz curtains originally designed for windows much larger than yours that tempts you to consider opting for a shabby chic bedroom. What do you do with this kind of legacy? You must experiment. Now is your chance to luxuriate in quantities of antique fabric that would otherwise be totally out of your financial reach. Indeed, if you have none, you should search for antique curtains that you can use for bed hangings as well as for your windows; alternatively you could unstitch them and transform your bed by making a new bed cover with a half tester, or adapt them to drape in great swathes over a simple four-poster frame. If there is still fabric over at the end, you could cover a cushion or re-upholster that little chair: well-worn fabric will never look brash or out of place.

Employing strong and impressive pieces of furniture in a bedroom can be more difficult because they can take over a room. Any reservations you might have about mixing antique with modern furniture should be dispelled if you choose pieces of similar line and proportion. You can emphasize this visual link by employing a distressed paint finish or an appropriate fabric to unify the various items. A linen press or *armoire* is ideal for clothes storage, and just right for a shabby chic look, but if bedroom space is at a premium, perhaps it will have to stand on a landing – an item of furniture to be admired.

Shabby chic is ideal for wandering travellers who arrive home from exotic lands laden with ethnic acquisitions; these textiles and objects tend to combine much more happily with faded and worn furniture and textiles than with brand-new upholstery and a selfconsciously designed scheme. For the budget-conscious decorator, for whom buying a property stretches resources to the limit, shabby chic can conserve funds. You can still put together a wonderfully theatrical effect. You can make a considered decision not to invest in 'bright and shiny new' but to celebrate 'well-built and old' instead. What does it matter that an arm of a chair is worn or that your sagging shelves are propped up on piles of books? The chair must be comfortable, and a straight line is less important than surrounding yourself with books.

The overall look of shabby chic, from subtly coloured distempered, peeling walls to big, cosy furniture that seems to have been there for ever, even the mellow lighting, is inviting; the room feels well lived-in.

FANTASTIC BEGINNINGS

Creating your own particular style depends to a certain degree on the furniture and accessories you have available. Few people are likely to inherit a wonderful four-poster bed, and yet they can be constructed in varying shapes and sizes from all sorts of odds and ends. Remember that in a poorly proportioned room a four-poster can appear dumpy, stealing what little height a room may have. Assuming that you do have the space, however, four-poster beds can be constructed from wood or metal, from DIY kits – even scaffolding poles. Once the frame is *in situ*, you can experiment with curtain permutations: formal and fixed, tied with ribbons, or unfinished lengths of fabric just thrown or draped – a constantly moving feast of ideas and whims. In this French château, the relative simplicity of the bed frame is disguised by the prodigious lengths of rough linen draped loosely over the poles, while an ancient narrow serving table at the foot of the bed bears candle and leather-bound volumes to further the fantasy. Why not try to create your own fairytale world!

MEDITERRANEAN

In a hot climate, interior decoration in the bedroom tends towards the minimal. The use of fabrics is negligible and more practical than decorative, with mosquito netting as bed hangings and cotton voile or calico curtains or blinds at the windows. Painted shutters will protect from sun and rain alike, the slats casting long and interesting shadows on bare walls and floors during the heat of the day. Furniture tends to be of bleached or pale wood, floors either scrubbed or tiled, and beds of a simple local construction, whether of wood, rattan or wrought iron.

Whitewash abounds, but dramatically juxtaposed with bright blue, yellow and pink highlights that bleach in the sun's heat to produce softer, quieter, faded shades which are more suitable for bedrooms than the bolder, brighter versions that preceded them.

Natural reds and oranges are popular too – terracotta colours that characterize those refreshing, tiled floors you find all over the Mediterranean. Marble, stone and wood are equally typical and easy to build into your design.

In a Mediterranean-inspired bedroom, arrestingly shaped bits of driftwood might gather as trophies on mantelpieces and window sills, along with fragile shells and seaside pebbles polished in rough waves – muted echoes of the bright outside world in a simple and uncluttered interior, essential for keeping cool.

This tranquil, underfurnished style of bedroom is ideal in the heat of the summer, but might lack in cosiness in winter, despite central heating. Plan for this in advance and incorporate a degree of flexibility: seasonal bed covers, for example, and curtains you can remove for the summer.

Warm climates encourage simplicity of style. In this refreshing, pared-down bedroom, the bed itself is uncomplicated by a frame. The fine mosquito net above it serves both a decorative and a functional purpose and the blind against the window has a similar translucency. The walls, ceiling and floor have been limewashed, together with the small chest and even the frame of the picture beside the bed. The model boat, the painting and the portholed shutters laid against the far wall combine to strike a cool, nautical note.

MODERN

A bedroom with a modern theme means there can be no half measures in its application. A style which relies heavily on structure and form and a significant use of space needs only one or two strong elements to enforce it. Stylish storage systems will help to emphasize the theme by preventing inappropriate belongings from upsetting the balance, while flooring can make a positive contribution to the design: use sympathetic colours, textures and finishes, or combine materials, such as wooden boards or even cement, polished to a marble finish, with rugs to soften the effect.

In a room where little is left on view, texture can play an important visual role. Fabrics for bed covers and even the bed linen can be made to toe the modern line.

While paintings may be out of financial range in the early years of property ownership, prints and black and white photographs are becoming increasingly popular. Alternatively, an interesting empty frame can give a wall a three-dimensional quality, while the strategic use of mirrors or even a strong architectural shape – a piece of furniture or free-standing sculpture, be it a 'find' or intended for display – can add interest in a dead corner.

Modern can be romantic as well as minimal. Here a small, low chair upholstered in fresh white linen with a silvery metallic appliqué, and a day bed, simply draped in a lace sheet and scattered with a few white-clad cushions, combine to sharpen up a fairly empty room. The pale blue tone of this corner, the transparency of the long, blue curtain, the drunken chandelier and the empty, ornate frame perched on the mantelpiece lend the room an air of mystery. The fireplace surround has been clad in reflective beaten metal, which gives the room another dimension. The overall effect is stylish, the minimum of possessions creating the maximum effect.

It takes great discipline to live in a modern interior. The architect John Pawson has designed this bedroom (far left) with the bed on a simple raised wooden platform, the warmth of the wood contrasting with the stark whiteness of the rest of the room. A row of recessed cupboards (closets) along one wall hints at orderly ranks of sharply pressed shirts and disciplined suits, racks of colour-coordinated shoes and pigeon holes for socks and knitwear. There are no bedside tables, no chairs, no mirrors or paintings to distract you from the minimalist look, the only concession to comfort being the soft duvet over the bed. The lighting has also been used to enhance the strictly architectural emphasis of this bedroom: strip lights run the length of the cupboards (closets) with additional wall strips behind the bed recess. The introduction of an Anglepoise lamp for reading is a surprisingly classic touch.

OUTDOORS

Sleeping out-of-doors requires few props, irrespective of how grand and memorable an occasion you wish it to be. A sleeping bag beside the dying embers of a picnic camp fire under the stars at the end of a mellow evening; a simple cotton hammock strung up between two trees, their spreading branches sheltering the incumbent from the afternoon sun; a tent in the back garden – all spontaneous suggestions that are instantly achievable.

Themed tents and special beds can be hired for one-time occasions. There is also a whole range of campaign furniture available – beds, tables, even wardrobes (closets) that derive from Napoleon's original designs. He wanted to be surrounded on the battlefield by familiar and, above all, comfortable furniture, designed to be collapsible and to fit into special trunks for ease of transportation. Authentic campaign furniture is rare, but it is quite possible to find inexpensive alternatives that will create the right feeling in your tented summer holiday quarters.

In an attempt to recapture something of the spirit and adventure encapsulated in Karen Blixen's novel *Out of Africa*, recreated so memorably by Sydney Pollack for the big screen, it is increasingly fashionable to take to canvas on exclusive wildlife safaris. The *frisson* of excitement or terror which results from being separated from a prowling night predator by only a thin expanse of canvas, coupled with the pure romance of eating outdoors by the light of a flickering storm lantern, listening to the noises of the bush, has to be the experience of a lifetime.

TOUCHING THE HEAVENS

The romanticism of sleeping in the open
air surrounded by diaphanous clouds of
mosquito netting, structured in the
shape of a tent, surely cannot be
bettered. Low camp beds on a floor of
rush matting share a bedside table in the
form of a campaign folding stool, with a
paraffin lamp and a cup of sweet-
smelling jacaranda standing on it. This
outdoor bedroom in Kenya is enclosed
only by the roof of the world, a
multitude of tiny stars penetrating the
netting of its transparent shelter in the
dark. It is certainly an exotic, glamorous
setting, but there is no reason why the
same effect cannot be reproduced
anywhere on a steamy summer's night.
Sleeping under the stars is an experience
not to be missed and generally it is not
difficult in practical terms to set up. So
exchange the security of your bed for a
night in the back garden – you will be
amazed by the plethora of stars.

DECORATION

The bedroom can occupy more or less any room in the house, from the tiniest shoe box to the airiest attic. Whether its look is spartan or luxurious, the bed will naturally play the starring role, its style and shape dictating the whole tone of the room. It is the happy combination, however, of paint and wallpaper, fabrics old and new, rugs or simple floorboards, wicker baskets or built-in cupboards – even Granny's chest of drawers given a new lease on life – that gives a room its intensely personal nature.

DECORATIVE PLANNING

That feeling of wanting to stamp your own personality upon your surroundings in exactly the way you would like, whether you are renting a room or have bought your own house, can often be frustrated by a shortfall in means. However, with very little expense and practically no expertise, a room can be transformed by a single pot of paint or a length of fabric.

Decorating never fails to take longer than you think, especially if you have little or no experience, so allow enough time to complete the job and reinstall the furniture before inviting your friends around for dinner and an inspection of your work. Try to finish the project in daylight; you will be surprised what a difference it makes if you work in good light.

You are probably more likely to encounter problems if you take on a more unusual site. You may be restrained by planning permission or the need for appropriate interior colour schemes in a period property, or the size or proportions of your rooms in a cottage in the country. Or you may be working on a space with quirky

architecture, a former warehouse perhaps, or a self-consciously modern and minimalist apartment. With so many constraints, it would be best to consult a professional with specialist knowledge, in the early stages in particular, because 'going it alone' is likely to become a minefield.

Every time you move, your bedroom is almost bound to change in character. In fact, as different architectural styles will reinterpret the same style in very different ways, it is unlikely that you will want to retain the same scheme when you move. Your sense of colour, style and coordination will develop and improve each time you decorate a room, however, just as your knowledge and experience grows, giving you more and more confidence to experiment with original and imaginative themes.

Colour and texture

Although paint is probably the first option, you can use paper or fabric to cover walls and ceiling, and you can cover your chairs and the bed – anything you choose, in

It is not just the bold colour scheme but also the use of different textures – on the wall, the bedhead and on the edges of the duvet and pillows – that brings this small bedroom to life (left).

An orange tone has been used to great effect in this unusual bedroom (right). The walls have been treated to resemble old plaster, with the dado, door and wall panelling picked out in complimentary cream and terracotta. The bed gives the room a modern feel; the strangely knotted bed cover and the painting of a dancing dog above it add a lighthearted touch. The painted screen may well hide a small washbasin or a rack of clothes.

Checks abound on walls, at windows, and on furniture in this tiny room (previous page, left). Designer Mimmi O'Connell has coordinated walls, ceiling and the detailing of the blinds in the same fabric. A small bed just fits laterally across the room, allowing a bright checked armchair to occupy the remaining space.

A small lamp uses a pretty chair as a side table (previous page, right), the ornament on its shade picking up a detail from the back of the chair.

SIMPLE COUNTRY EFFECTS

**Simplicity in decoration is always
effective. In this rustic bedroom, with its
low ceiling and thick, uneven walls,
decoration has been kept to the bare
minimum. The bulk of a somewhat solid,
unforgiving carved wooden bed is
relieved only by an upright painted chair
beside it and a narrow cotton runner on
the scrubbed, wooden floor. However,
the walls have been washed in a
pretty yellow, instead of being left
whitewashed, which offsets the austerity
that characterizes the furnishings,
The bold use of a contrasting darker
colour below an imaginary dado level
emphasizes the warmth of the yellow
above and improves the proportions
of this little room.**

fact – with checks or stripes, with traditional floral chintz or with just plain colours. Texture plays a very important role, coordinating not only colours but also combinations of patterns and fabrics: flat cottons with slub silks, appliqué and lace – even a soft, old, worn paisley shawl.

Choosing the dominant colour for your bedroom is a matter of courage. If you have inherited a tired set of walls, or a room papered in some ghastly pattern, you will be obliged either to strip everything down and paper it, or to conceal such horrors by covering them up with a dark colour. Choose a colour that complements or echoes a favourite painting or bedspread, or a piece of painted furniture that will be housed in the room.

It is worth poring over a practical decorating book before you decide anything, in order to look at examples of all the different effects you might want to achieve, be it with paint, wallpaper or fabric; to learn how easy or hard they will be to effect; and to understand fully the problems and advantages of each. It is very easy to choose the wrong paint, or to paint where wallpaper would have been better.

WARM WOOD

Pine panelling is typical of Alpine chalet architecture. Its warm yellow tones can be rather overwhelming, precluding the use of many bright, primary colours for bed linen and furnishing fabrics. Carved features, columns or detailing define the panels on the wooden walls. Enhance the natural beauty of the grain of the wood, its whorls and idiosyncracies, by varnishing, staining or even colour-washing walls and floors. You can incorporate more wood in the furnishing of the room with turned wooden lamp stands with pale shades, for instance, or hang simply framed paintings on the panelling – perhaps contrasting woodgrain and patina for additional texture. A glorious antique painted wardrobe (closet) would add the final touch, or you may want to paint your own modern equivalent.

With a low ceiling, the size of the bed is important. The brass finials of the four-poster touch the ceiling, but the frame has been left bare in order not to exaggerate the lack of space. Instead, the eye moves instantly away from the ceiling to the pretty white lace bed cover and crisp duvets.

Wallpaper is a traditional wall treatment; if the previous occupant of your bedroom left walls full of cracks and holes, wallpaper is an easy and effective cover-up.

Stripes provide a solid base for the decoration of any room (opposite), but ensure that the room is square, or your lines will not end up straight. If you are papering a small room, striped wallpaper will help to disguise its size.

A plain paper is useful if you are dealing with uneven or lumpy walls. Paint applied over the paper will reveal fewer of the damaged patches. When you have finished, any spare paper left over could be used to re-cover old hat boxes to make decorative storage units.

Look at the age of your room first; it may have a bearing on how you proceed. For example, although you will have to kerb your rasher impulses, and decorating a period property authentically can be an exacting exercise, it can also be quite stimulating, and there are now a vast number of heritage paints – period colours and paint recipes – on the market to make a successful job easier. If you do wish to pursue this option in your bedroom, there are umpteen books on the subject to offer advice on all the relevant areas: architectural detailing, wall colours, curtain and furnishing styles – appropriate patterns and fabrics too.

Modern rooms tend to be less demanding. It is not unusual to encounter unfinished walls in a warehouse context and you can exploit the textures of raw breeze blocks, bricks, rough metal supports and cement walls to advantage if you incorporate them into a simple bedroom design. Tall ceilings and large rooms provide ample area for trial and error and, with an emphasis on space, your possessions can happily take on gigantic proportions.

Big needs to be bold, so you cannot be tentative. Dramatic colours, bold designs on bare walls, or a commitment to a smart, monochrome theme: without historical constraints, this is perhaps the closest you will come to being given true freedom to express yourself. If you do choose pale, less overwhelming colour schemes, they are likely to benefit from accents of colour: decorative

FLEXIBLE FABRIC

Fabric is an adaptable wall covering that can be used very successfully in a wide variety of rooms. More formally, the fabric would be battened: narrow strips of wood would be tacked onto the wall as a base onto which the lengths of material would be attached. This produces an effect similar to wallpaper, although the texture and colour combinations of fabrics create a softer and often warmer atmosphere.

Hanging fabric loosely around the four walls like curtains creates an interesting textural effect; here (left) the lengths of crisp, white cotton hang in unregulated folds, from a narrow bamboo pole which runs around the room, tied by short lengths of matching fabric. Its effect is immediately to soften the harsh austerity of the box structure of the room and to avoid the need for any additional accessories in the shape of mirrors, pictures, etc., as these would be difficult to hang successfully on folds of material.

details, such as wall hangings, paintings or mirrors, a bright bed cover or an interesting bedhead will fulfil this brief.

If you are working in a rustic environment, steer clear of those dark, vibrant colours that work well in the city: with low ceilings and small windows, rooms will begin to resemble dungeons. Keep colours light and bright and keep the whole scheme simple. Either paint beams, picking up a tone used for window frames to tie the whole scheme together, or to lend emphasis to the ceiling, or stain them to bring out the wood's grain and natural colour.

If you are decorating or restoring a panelled room, it may be difficult to replicate the original wood – almost impossible if it is antique. A *trompe l'oeil* paint effect executed by an expert will probably come closest; or you might like to brighten up the panelling by painting it. You could even create simple mock-panelling on a blank wall.

Above all, experiment, for bravery brings rewards: using bright, clashing colours might create a surprisingly exciting bedroom environment. If it proved disastrous, you would only have to repaint the walls or buy a new set of less outrageous sheets.

Flooring

Spend time and money on flooring; it is an important and often neglected aspect of a decorative scheme. A uniform floor covering can offer a continuity of flow between a series of rooms or, if you choose wildly differing styles and colours on the walls of different rooms, can pull the overall design scheme together. If expense is a factor, you can leave plain wooden floors, or put down coir or seagrass matting throughout to provide a natural background for individual rugs and kelims, chosen for each room.

COSY CARPETS

Carpets tend to be one of the first things you replace when you move. In many cases they are laid wall to wall to disguise the indifferent surface of the floor underneath, but it is a good idea to check on the condition of the floorboards, as many are in surprisingly good shape and an industrial sander would soon have the surface smooth and splinter-free. If you are lucky enough to discover a proper parquet floor (left), a good polish is all that is required to bring it up to scratch. Other wooden floors may not be quite so easily salvaged, in which case you might consider painting the floor – either in a deep gloss or with a pale Scandinavian-style wash. Then you need only throw a few loose rugs on top – kelims or Indian dhurries, for example.

Otherwise you could choose a carpet that will provide the main decorative theme of the bedroom. A carpet resembling jaguar fur brightens up the quiet modernity of this room (right) and has been used to cover the platform base of the bed as well. The strength of its statement means that other elements pale into insignificance: bold white for the duvet cover is safe.

Visually, a wooden floor can provide pattern and texture, depending on how it is laid. Tiles, marble slabs and even bricks can add interest in a less traditional style of bedroom but, as all these materials are cold to the touch, it is probably worth scattering them with carpets, runners, rugs, and innovative floorcoverings for comfort's sake. Bedroom floors need to be cosy; that first toe needs to be tempted out of bed in the morning.

There are paint varieties on the market that are actually recommended for floors – hard-wearing enough to sustain scuffing and scratches. So you could design your own kelim and paint it on the floor of your bedroom, and then the colour scheme of the floor could reflect the tones of other objects and textiles in the room, without the need for a long-winded and expensive search for a proper rug. More simply, you could paint the floor a dark, high gloss – you will be amazed how it changes the atmosphere.

Do not forget more traditional forms of floor covering. You can use strong colours or patterns in a carpet as the leading element in a decorative scheme, choosing fabrics and wall finishes to coordinate with it, rather than the other way round. If you only own moth-eaten rugs, you can still create an opulent effect by overlapping them on your floor Middle-Eastern fashion, ensuring that the good part of one covers the holes in another. You should be able to cover most of the floor with minimal cost and effort.

Window dressing

Practically speaking, when money is any sort of consideration, there is little that you can do with the structure of the windows you inherit with your property, but there is no shortage of exciting and imaginative ways –

both simple and elaborate – in which you can disguise, dress, or emphasize their form from the inside. Consider all the alternatives rather than limiting yourself to traditional treatments straight away.

The function of window dressing is primarily protective – insulating you from the prying eyes of the outside world – and many people do indeed resort to pinning an old sheet or blanket up against their bedroom window when they first move into a room. It may stay a while because finding more permanent protection is a crucial step that should not be hurried; your choice will play an important part in the overall decorative scheme of the room, so be sure rather than investing in fabric and fittings that do not look right.

Different window treatments can change the atmosphere of a room dramatically. In this distinctly summer bedroom (above) a single voile curtain hangs from an unobtrusive wrought-iron pole over each French window. It billows in the gentle breeze but does not change the quality of sunlight entering the room.

The tiny window above this neat bed under the eaves (right) would be dwarfed by the addition of curtains. Arched shutters shaped to fit the rounded window take up little space and could reveal a painted mural – a moon and stars perhaps, or a pastoral scene – when closed.

BEAUTIFUL BLINDS

For many people living in large cities, being visible to neighbours is a constant problem. New and exciting decorative ideas have now been explored, however, that can replace the twitching net curtains so often turned to as a last resort in the past.

You can hang translucent blinds, made of cotton voile, or sheeting, or anything pale that lets in the light, from the top of the window frame in your bedroom to cover the window permanently. When you have two or three old sash windows in the room hang a blind at each, so that you can raise and lower them independently as you wish, according to the amount of light required.

The decorative theme of the windows can be extended by hanging a similar length of fabric as a wall hanging behind the bed. Oriental-style stencils in gold on each blind (right) can also create a striking window covering, reinforced by the central motif on the white cotton bedspread; the lamp base and wide shade pursue the theme. The overall decorative effect is that of soft, filtered light, cocooning the bedroom and successfully shutting out the world beyond.

Many period properties retain their traditional internal shutters which, on top of their decorative potential, provide additional security. However, when closed at night the bare wood may be look dull. Lliven up the shutters by tacking bright tin or even copper to them, or paint a pastoral or moonlit scene on them to gaze at from the bed.

If you live in a basement and your bedroom gets little or no light, you could exaggerate this to dramatic effect. Instead of putting up expensive curtains, intersperse the standard, clear glass panes with coloured glass or, even

simpler, stick a coloured gel across the window pane. The glass can be decorated in other ways too: frosted, engraved with an interesting motif, or covered in an opaque rice paper that has been cut ornamentally. Daylight would be filtered and soft, casting gentle shadows over the interior of the room – ideal for a room with no view.

Blinds are very useful for awkward windows but are sometimes considered rather a poor solution in a bedroom, compared with warm, voluptuous curtains. Given an original and individual treatment, however, painted with scenes, or cut with a pattern of holes so that sunshine or street light will illuminate the motif, making it glow with life, a parchment blind can be a very decorative feature.

With blinds of natural materials such as rattan, bamboo and cane, which allow the sunlight to filter through the loose weave, you could add an edging in a fabric that matches the bed cover, or the upholstery of the bedroom chair, for a more coordinated decorative effect. Instead of adjusting the blinds traditionally with a simple cord, you could fix them permanently in one position with ties in the same edging material or in a coordinating colour.

More austere Venetian blinds suit modern spaces; they can be wooden and kept natural, or painted, or even more sophisticated. You can then control the amount of light allowed into the room and adjust it according to the prevailing weather conditions.

Ultimately, fabric will always be by far the most flexible raw material for dressing windows. Choose the design and the material at the same time as you are planning the colour of your bed linen and walls. Curtains can sweep dramatically and fall luxuriously, and do not have to be complicated to make.

Furnishing fabrics are surprisingly cheap and come in widths appropriate for large-scale ideas. It is important to remember, when measuring, that to match stripes and patterns will require considerably more fabric than your initial measurements might suggest; you must also allow for a certain amount of shrinkage. Either take into account a possible 10 per cent shrinkage and cut accordingly, or wash the material before you start to cut it into lengths. This first wash should also dispose of any stiffening in the fabric and make it easier to work with.

WINDOW DRESSING

If your bedroom is not architecturally interesting, make a special feature of the window: a little can go a long way.

Not all translucent curtains have to be white or ivory. Indeed, this fabric (left, above) comprising pale blue-and-white checks, allows quite a lot of light to filter through. It has been gathered into curtains and fixed permanently in place across the bay window, tied with matching fabric to create a fuller shape. The table in front of the centre window is draped in a coordinating blue-and-white striped cotton, and stacked with tiers of fabric-covered boxes, flanked by tall lamps that pick up the blue theme.

Curtains and window treatments for skylights and awkwardly placed windows in lofts or under the eaves, where window shapes tend not to be standard, can pose problems. Roller blinds can satisfy this requirement but tend to be pretty basic. Alternatively, you could introduce some sturdy plants (left, below) to act as a screen, or use them in conjunction with a blind. Your decorative theme would influence the style and colour of the pots and the plants would provide additional pleasure and colour if they produced flowers or fruit.

CLEVER DISGUISE

Accessorizing the bedroom is probably more fun than anywhere else in the house. The variety of bed linen, pillows and cushions, blankets, duvets, throws and rugs on the market today means that you can basically change the look of your bedroom every time you change the sheets. You can have plain, striped, checked or patterned sheets or duvet cover in all the colourways imaginable, with coordinated blankets and even lamp bases and lampshades to match. If you are more ambitious, you might dress up that anonymous side table in a check or stripe to complement the week's bed linen. In fact, who is to know that there is a table under there at all? Many a serviceable table has been revealed as an upturned cardboard box cleverly draped in fabric!

A successful scheme does not always have to be an immaculate mix and match combination, however. You can play around with your existing bed linen, rejuvenate ancient blankets by sewing a colourful cotton border around the fraying edges and go through Granny's trunk searching for old patchwork quilts and pretty embroidered bedspreads that would add the finishing touch.

Few bedrooms have the space to house a dressing table as a specific piece of furniture, and in essence it is an old-fashioned notion; but the necessity of a set of drawers for those small, personal items and a flat surface for a good mirror is still high on the agenda.

Unusually shaped bedrooms sometimes incorporate strange niches, often either side of a chimney breast or in a former fireplace, which can be exploited to advantage. Position a stray table, preferably with a couple of drawers in it, to fit into the alcove, and add a lace tablecloth. Delicate reading lamps and a pretty, decorative mirror will complete the picture, while all those bowls of rings and bracelets, keys, pens, hairbands and bows that invariably go missing for want of a more permanent home will add that final, personal, finishing touch.

If you do not find formal curtain-making an appealing prospect, there are plenty of other ways to hang fabric. The haberdashery department of any big store is like an Aladdin's cave of loops, curtain rings and eyelets of every conceivable metal and material; colourful arrays of braid of all descriptions with matching tassels; ribbons of widely differing textures and shades. All you need is a little imagination and the courage of your convictions.

Equally, if making curtains is beyond you, the old blanket tacked to the window frame can be replaced by a more dramatic alternative until you have discovered a seamstress. Last summer's faded sarongs will liven up your windows with their unusual colours and designs. Or a tea towel might fit a narrower window. Instead of tacking it to the wall, you could add a degree of permanence by punching brass eyelets into the two top corners, to hang the tea towel from hooks screwed into the window frame.

If you want to be more unorthodox, experiment with a simple curtain pole: try draping your fabric over the curtain pole and playing around with the general fullness of the swags – curtain fabric can be quite stiff but cotton voile or lengths of mosquito netting will hang beautifully. Finials can be added afterwards to complete the look.

Street lights are often a problem, if you are an urban dweller: even lined curtains do a poor job of keeping out the glare in the small hours of the morning. Hotels use blackout blinds which are concealed by day behind smart dress curtains; a double set of curtains might also solve the problem, and would prove less austere in your own bedroom. Alternatively, you could cover a screen and put that in the window to block out the light or simply move a cheval glass or similarly tall piece of furniture into position.

Furniture and fittings

When you come to furnishing your bedroom, you will be using your imagination and creative assets at maximum capacity. With your basic colour scheme now firmly in place, and the proposed treatment of walls, windows and floors agreed, the selection and arrangement of your furniture and the fine-tuning of your own accessories will require thought and discipline.

SCREENED OFF

The soft furnishings in a bedroom contribute in large part to the personal atmosphere that is ultimately created. Although nothing is standard and beds can come in a wide range of styles and sizes, it is the way the pieces of furniture are pulled together; the use of fabrics and colours to soften their edges; and the introduction of new ideas that ensures the final look's overall success.

Here, in what might be considered by some a slightly gloomy bedroom, there is an all-embracing tranquillity, making it the perfect resting place at the end of a stress-filled day. The narrow metal twin beds are painted an interesting pale blue-grey, their striped covers echoing the blue of the bed frames. There are no cushions, however, to break the line at the head of the bed, no light touch on the side table, no flowers, no sense of levity.

The folding screens on one side of each bed, their wrought-iron frames threaded with lengths of white broderie anglaise with a pretty scalloped edge, are both decorative and functional, shielding the occupant against draughts and providing an essential sense of enclosure and privacy.

You may have decided on a new bed. As the one essential item in any bedroom, spare no expense. There are many aspects to consider when you buy a bed (see page 60), not merely its style and size.

Apart from the bed, there is no absolute need for any other furniture in the bedroom, although if you have space available, a bedside table, a comfortable reading chair and stylish, effective storage for all your clothes and personal belongings are all luxuries that could be incorporated into a decorative scheme to advantage.

If your bedroom is very small or a difficult shape for some of your furniture, then you will have to adapt. A chest of drawers with a small mirror perched on it can replace a dressing table. Tables, whether round or square, are good corner fillers: the flat surface can be used for books, a vase of flowers, ornaments, photographs or other personal items and, if you drape it in a coordinated fabric or an antique oddment, it can liven up a dead corner and can conceal boxes of junk beneath the folds.

Beautiful old wardrobes (closets) are can be expensive; they can be cumbersome; very few fit easily into a bedroom and many appear even heavier than they are because of the rich colour of the polished wood. You could, however, look for a smaller, cheaper cupboard (closet), which you could paint as an integral part of your decorative scheme. You could add a chair in the same tone, too. A fabric tent, constructed around a simple frame across the corner of a room, could also provide space to conceal clothes and overnight bags without dominating the room visually. Just like a Victorian changing tent on a beach, this self-styled wardrobe (closet) can blend into its surroundings or take centre stage, depending on how elaborately you dress it.

Storage and display

Try not to over-clutter your space because the fewer pieces of furniture you put in a room, the larger it will appear, and the bed will already take up a substantial proportion of the available room. If you have a low ceiling, leave the walls free of large paintings and mirrors as these will draw attention to it. Accessories should be kept small and simple, too: a few pictures or photographs by the bed, a sampler, or even a few pretty plates on the wall.

How you choose to display your favourite things can play as large a part in the overall decoration of your bedroom as the paint and fabric. Ultimately, however, if you intend to drill the wall full of holes to display a vast array of pictures and photographs, you will not have to worry so much about the finish you achieve with your paintbrush. As the months go by, the pristine exhibition of frames will inevitably become augmented by flotsam picked up along the way: souvenirs of a recent trip will find a vantage point on the edge of a heavy mirror frame, together with postcards from friends; while hats, scarves, ties and handbags will nearly always end up perched on the knob of the bedstead or hooked on the edge of a picture.

Making collections of personal souvenirs can some-times take an obsessional turn but some of the more interesting trophies can be put to a practical purpose. Collections of colourful empty tins could be used for storage, for anything from coins to safety pins, while antique luggage, which has become highly collectable, especially grand leather suitcases embossed with some stranger's initials and lined in green silk, can be piled up in a prominent position to act not only as a decorative focus, but also as containers for your spare bed linen and blankets. A leather trunk at the foot of the bed could be filled with all those difficult things that you can never store tidily, like maps, unruly electrical cable, and maddeningly shaped baskets, while magazines and books – even last night's discarded clothes – could rest on the top.

Decorating ideas are constantly changing, although at a different rate to the volatile fashion world, and there will always be a new look to try. Decorating trends move backwards and forwards from exotic to minimalist, from dark, vibrant colours to pastel and natural tones, from opulent to austere. As in the fashion world, however, an over-enthusiastic adherence to a new trend can sometimes prove an expensive mistake. Be careful.

The bed in this spacious attic (right) has been positioned at an angle, taking up more room than it would otherwise. The sloping walls and jutting roof beams restrict the possibility of other furniture and the only item on display is the oval mirror on its wrought-iron stand, which occupies a prominent position in the middle of the floor.

The layout of your bedroom depends entirely on the number of possessions you like, and need, to have around you. And a lack of storage space may mean that some of your belongings have to be on display so you must be extremely orderly.

In contrast to the more self-conscious attic space, this bedroom of normal proportions loudly proclaims the personality of its owner (right), even to providing clues to his initials emblazoned in red above the bed. Although average in size, this room has been given over to a conscious display of eclectic bits and pieces: a curious collection of framed chequer boards and coats of arms, a snooker score board and a shelf of childhood toys. At the foot of the bed, valuable space is occupied by a low wooden stool bearing four large cylindrical tins, which could house socks, underwear, or any other useful things.

As purposeful as this room is in its display, the storage elements of those more private possessions must be equally so. At the opposite end of the room to the bed is a built-in cup-board (closet), glimpsed briefly in one of the horizontal mirrors that hang above the bed.

DECORATING TIPS

- Have the courage of your own convictions. Don't be inclined to ask too many friends' advice. A bedroom designed by committee will not be a success.
- Start with one strong element of colour, whether floor-covering, textile or item of furniture, and let that influence your overall design.
- Register any problem areas before you get too involved. An expert's opinion and help at the beginning will save time and tears later.
- Don't despair of your furniture – an indifferent wardrobe (closet) or worn blanket box can be scrubbed, painted, stencilled or just disguised to give a new and more appropriate look.
- Take time over the details of your decorative theme. Specific ideas often take longer to come together and it is worth waiting for the right fabric or other element, rather than cutting corners, to achieve the best effect.
- Never throw anything away until after your bedroom has come together. You may find that the very item you so eagerly disposed of during the initial turn out is the very thing needed to finish off your new image.

FURNISHING
THE BED

In any bedroom, the bed takes centre stage. And whether formal and tailored or soft and casual, the bedroom is the place where fabric can be used to convey a sense of sophistication and elegance, or warmth and comfort; the secret lies in the blend of colours and textures of bed linen and fabrics.

Bed curtains or drapery, country quilts, pillowcases and duvet covers, fine linen or pure cotton sheets – all have a decorative potential when you come to furnish the bed.

MAKING CHOICES

The universally accepted fact that the majority of us spend one third of our lives in bed underlines the importance of finding the right mattress. Hand-made mattresses can be ordered to fit any shape and configuration of bed, new or antique, while a range of mass-produced styles can be tried and tested for size and comfort in showrooms everywhere. It is essential – in the interests of a good night's sleep – to have a good bounce on a mattress before you buy it.

It is equally important to search out the right pillows and in today's allergy-conscious society,

feathers may be a problem. It is wise to check what the pillows are filled with and to test the relative comfort/support of the different types available. Pillows of different shapes in various colourways and combinations can create interest on a simple bed with a plain headboard, or one that has to be jammed against the wall. There are square versions called Oxford pillows as well as the

standard oblong variety. And then there is a huge range of smaller cushions, be they tapestry or lace, circular, square or heart-shaped, ornamental or just comforting, possibly filled with fragrant lavender or sleep-inducing remedies – personal touches with a decorative edge.

Finding the correct duvet and trying to understand variable tog (density) values and the different merits of different filling products is just one more challenge. Moreover, you may still prefer to be tucked into sheets and blankets, for there is just nothing quite like slipping into wonderful starched, crisp linen sheets. Freshly laundered linen, and traditional wool blankets edged with satin, must still be the ultimate in luxury. Although the ubiquitous duvet seems to have relegated blankets to second place, they still make a cosy bed. If you prefer neatness, a duvet has a habit of looking perpetually untidy, whereas blankets tuck firmly under the mattress with sharp, mitred corners.

FRESH TO FORMAL

Beds come in all shapes and sizes. Wicker beds are an unusual feature (previous page, left), the warmth of their natural colour accentuated by a predominant use of red in this otherwise simple Balearic bedroom. A four-poster bed, by contrast, in a small room, makes an imposing and altogether less flexible impression. Simple beds, like this pretty wrought-iron framed example (far left), can be made to appear softer with a squashy duvet and an abundance of pillows.

Bed linen nearly always comes in a variety of colourways: a large blue-and-white check alternated with striped blue-and-white and plain white pillowcases, with a variety of blue edgings, gives the bed a freshness you can almost smell. You might create a more exciting effect by mixing the colours – perhaps red-and-white with yellow-and-white pillowcases instead of more traditional blue combinations.

A traditional four-poster bed with festooned bedhangings creates a more formal decorative style (left), here tempered by the lightness of the bamboo-style posts, complemented by the bamboo bench at its foot, and the simple white cotton bed cover.

■ 5 9

Whatever the bed and wherever it is situated, you can disguise a tired look if you use fabric cleverly. You can transform an occasional guest bed in the study into a day bed if it is covered with a smart tartan rug with a few cushions scattered on it. Colourful cotton dhurries or light kelims introduce a novel texture; they can be used to great effect as bed covers, while patterned paisley, silk saris and other ethnic fabrics give any bed an exotic feel.

The bedstead

If you are buying a bed for the first.time, you may be uncertain as to what to look for. Divan-style beds are the most readily available; they come with or without a headboard. The advantage of this type of bed is its accessibility, for although it may be unimaginative to walk into a showroom and buy your bed 'off the peg', as it were, you do, at least, have a chance to try out the different styles, testing the length and width of each bed, the degree of support, and looking carefully at any other factors which will affect your final decision.

Antique beds tend to be small when compared to the vast 6ft (183cm) king-size beds available today in the shops. If you are tall or share your bed with a large person, think twice before opting for a 4ft 6in (137cm) variety. If discussing this style it would be wise at the planning stage to include in your costings the price of a mattress, too.

Similarly, an authentic French *bateau lit* is almost bound to require a base and a mattress. This style of bed may prove well worth a big financial outlay, however, as it seems to suit masculine bed linen and romantic and whimsical drapery equally well, making it truly versatile – a lasting investment. The style is gaining widespread

popularity and modern reproduction versions are now being manufactured in standard sizes to meet this demand. If you decide on this Continental type, a duvet is essential, or making the bed will be a nightmare.

If you want to find a more interesting and more unusual option, it will take time. Everyone seems short of time today, but it may seem shorter still if you are spending sleepless nights on an old mattress on the floor while you search for the ultimate bed. If you are looking in an antique shop or at an auction, you will need a little imagination: brass and wrought-iron bedsteads are often hard to envisage as beds when seen out of context, stacked as

Another way to maintain the decorative drama of your bedroom if you are short of paintings and accessories is to emphasize the sense of colour coordination and focus attention on the bed itself, rather than on the room in general. Blue and white are two colours eternally linked and always popular. The interesting use of varying shades of blue on this bed – the two-tone headboard and contrasting blankets, dark blue pillowcases edged in white and even a blue trimming on the sheet – all compensate for a rather ordinary room.

DIAPHANOUS DREAMS

Fabrics can change the atmosphere of
any room, softening a spartan interior,
disguising its shortcomings and
harmonizing any rough edges. An
eclectic mix of materials and textiles will
bring out the best in any bedroom.

There is no feature in this room (left)
to distract your eye from a large expanse
of bed. The walls are without pictures,
there is no furniture, not even a lamp.
However, because of an appropriate
choice of wall colour and the gentle
combinations of the right fabric and
textures, the overall effect is one of
tranquillity, conducive to sleep. The pale
eau de nil of the walls sets a calm and
peaceful mood; the dreamy transparency
of the mosquito netting hanging from a
frame in the ceiling reinforces the effect.

The intricate patchwork quilt is
draped casually over the wide bed
disguising the disarray of unmade
blankets, and ticking pillowcases are
just visible. The bright Persian rug
provides a glowing block of colour on
the floor, yet its faded red tones are
not remotely intrusive.

■ 61

HEADBOARD HEAVEN

Styles of bed differ so much that the
term headboard may seem somehow
inaccurate. Many brass and iron beds
come with a top and a tail of differing
heights, four-posters are often without either, and a vast number of beds
simply improvize.

If you possess a mattress and a base
but no specific frame as such, you can
invent or design your own bedhead
(right). A set of disused shutters, a wall
hanging or an interesting rug would
provide a focus for the eye in the same
way, and would supply a new texture at
the same time. A large, unwieldy picture
in need of a home might be happy
standing against the wall behind the
mattress or hanging heavily above it.

Why not try using a screen, whether
clad in fabric, covered in postcards, or
just painted? Remember those Victorian
screens covered in a collage of images
and then varnished? It would also add a
very feminine touch as the surround for a
pretty guest bed, and you could expand
the idea by using chintz for the curtains
and bed cover, even a floral wallpaper.

heads and tails against the back wall of a shop. Remember to make sure that all the pieces are present and intact; that the iron runners which attach head to tail fit comfortably into the retaining section at each end, so that you do not find yourself on the floor again, with only ironwork for blankets and pillows.

If your bed-hunting proves fruitless, you can combine the possibility of tried and tested comfort with an imaginative setting, by buying the divan of your choice from a standard outlet, together with its mattress, and designing your own bed around it.

You need not limit yourself to personalizing the headboard; you could construct an entire frame. If you are not entirely happy about entrusting the safety of your prone body to your creation, ensure that the store-supplied base carries all the weight and that your homemade frame is free-standing around it.

Once again, junk shops and auctions will reveal a host of potential components: extraordinary bits of architectural salvage, furniture, columns, ironwork, paintings and posts. Fabric, ribbon, pieces of carpet, tassels and braid can be used to disguise any unattractive seams or areas which do not fit as neatly as they might. Odd lengths of silk and ethnic embroidery can be incorporated into the drapery of a four-poster bed. Things do not have to match; it is the overall effect that is important.

The headboard

If you lack the time or confidence to launch into a full-scale project, keep your ideas simple. You can still give your bed a personal touch if you choose to concentrate purely on the headboard and its surroundings. Design a mural, and

PERSONAL TOUCHES

A blank wall, even if laden with an interesting selection of pictures, can look rather conservative and unexciting. However, a strong image has been created in this case (left) by using a series of pen and ink drawings, all identically framed, above a wooden headboard which has been softened with a long flat cushion, upholstered in white cotton. As the piles of books either side of the bed would suggest, this headboard has been designed with an avid reader in mind.

Test your artistic talent and paint your own style of headboard onto the wall, as here (left). In this particular case, the design is little more than an outline, painted in a colour to match that of the blanket cover, its shape reflecting the design of the two lights on either side of the bed. What gives this bed an additional perspective is the stone wall above and behind the bed, which reinforces the colour scheme and provides a shelf at the same time. In cases like this, when the bed has been squeezed into a small space with no room either side for tables or even a chair, any thought of a bed frame has also had to be abandoned.

UNDER THE EAVES

Creating a very bold scheme is often the answer if you are dealing with restricted spaces or where the architecture dictates the limits of your design. In this masculine attic (left) a single four-poster has been constructed to fit in under the eaves. Although there is little space to be too elaborate, using contrasting checks here has proved very successful. Matching checked silk throws have been used as a bed cover and hanging while a larger check in different colours is used for the carpet. Using strong textiles has avoided the need to add very much decoration on the little wall space available.

This airy summer bedroom (right) by contrast, although also an attic space, has a high ceiling; architectural interest surrounds you, from the exposed rafters and old-fashioned ceiling fan, to the high window. Storage space above and within the curtained cupboards (closets) enclose a comfortable window seat. Seen through the filter of a mosquito net, the clapboard interior of the room is painted white throughout. White muslin curtains cover the cupboards (closets); the sheets, pillowcases and quilt are all white and blue.

If you are in the happy position of being able to rummage in the family blanket box to see what you can plunder, now is the time, for although there is always an abundance of new designs to suit any decorative scheme, the quality of some old linen and blankets is unbeatable, and deserves a little loyalty. Moreover, although the more practically minded of you will shudder at the idea of ironing – and starching – so many yards of sheeting, perhaps if you have resisted buying new linen, you should on this occasion take advantage of a local laundry service.

If you are short of a suitable cover for the top blanket, a lace tablecloth would make a pretty cover during the summer and can be replaced by a tartan travel blanket when the nights start to get cooler. If you are more concerned with a coordinated end result, why not design an interesting original bed cover – perhaps a patchwork using up scraps of curtain material, or a more sophisticated American-style quilt with a personal motif. You can pick up on colours or motifs from the linen when you come to cover your reading chair, perhaps, or if you have cushions on a window seat.

Some ideas for bed linen may be entirely original, while others may be inspired by a set from a period drama on the big screen or on television. Your own choice may be influenced by a display in a shop window, an imaginative photograph in a colour magazine or even by the acquisition of a particularly beautiful fabric. It is your interpretation of each of these trends that makes your bedroom personal, intuitive and fun. Whatever direction you choose to take, analyse the colour and pattern in schemes that you like, the contrasts of scale and proportion, and use this as your guide.

CHILDREN'S BEDROOMS

A very particular set of criteria come into play when you design a child's bedroom. You must place the emphasis on bright, bold fun, but be aware of the constant need for space and sufficient storage. An older child's bedroom should incorporate areas for more serious occupations and many children's beds nowadays build work and storage units into their general design, providing a vast array of adjustable shelving, drawer and table space – ideal when there is homework to do, or a computer to house.

STARTING OUT

Children are likely to spend a lot of time in their bedrooms. For those not fortunate enough to have a separate nursery or playroom, the room will have to assume a number of important roles. Primarily it is where the child sleeps, and there are beds to suit every child's fantasy. Some are disguised as buses and trams; modular beds incorporate writing areas, television and computer stations and sleeping platforms. Bunk beds will enable you to accommodate easily any unexpected guests, but truckle beds, inflatable mattresses or even camp beds can lend an impromptu stay a certain *frisson* of excitement.

Sleeping should be fun and planning the whole room around a favourite cartoon or television character is one way to create a sympathetic environment. Decorate the walls with cut-outs, posters and friezes, and retain the theme in your soft furnishings: bed linen today is developed to follow every new trend, so characters from literary classics and stars of the big screen appear on duvet covers, pillowcases and matching pyjamas to boot.

Children are acquisitive by nature and notoriously untidy, so storage must be near the top of any agenda in a child's room. They like to be able to see their toys, which means that increasingly, nowadays, the traditional toy box is being replaced by transparent plastic bins. If you make tidying up fun, you will encourage your child to help, so plan your storage carefully. Use bright and colourful units; keep shelving, boxes and drawers within easy reach. A bed with built-in drawers underneath is a popular solution to housing everything from clothes to toys; or big wicker baskets which are light enough for a child to move around.

TOY TOWN

A bright colourful room is always popular with a younger child, with an abundance of storage space to accommodate the ever-increasing number of toys. Remember to position shelves with the height of the child in mind, so that the games, puzzles and books that are used on a daily basis are always easily accessible. The bed should be big enough to accommodate both the child and a huge family of teddy bears, the overflow perhaps living in a painted trunk. The floor is another important feature of a child's room because many games happen at this level. It should be smooth and practical, avoiding the possibility of splinters in knees and hands, and for reasons of hygiene, but at the same time it should provide the optimum surface for car chases, battles and general high jinks.

It is unusual today to meet a child who is not fascinated by either the small screen or the cinema. If you intend to let your child have a television, insist that it is situated sufficiently high up to be out of harm's way; perhaps you could use the same shelf to store videos. Remember, too, that electricity can be lethal so wires should be inaccessible.

Nursery

One of the joys of expecting a baby is building a cosy nest for it. Although initially it will be unappreciative of your efforts, a baby's smile as it grows gradually more familiar with the colours and shapes in its bedroom will bring pleasure to everyone.

Plan the room to incorporate the essentials: cot (crib), grown-up's chair, changing mat and storage for clothes and nappies (diapers). Try not to take up valuable space with bulky chests of drawers. Instead, you could simply screw a hanging rail to the wall and suspend colourful plastic buckets from it, to keep everything in one area.

You might find the number of coordinated ranges of nursery wallpapers and fabrics overwhelming. They can be brightly primary-coloured or quietly pastel (less interesting for the baby but more peaceful for you), purely decorative or educational, featuring animals, clowns, flowers, or nursery rhymes. Or you can invent your own design.

The nursery of your first-born will be the object of infinite thought: not only the colour of the room but the position of the cot (crib), changing table, wardrobe (closet) and clothes rail will have been the focus of much agonizing. You may decide to employ an old-fashioned iron cot (crib) in a corner of the room (left) next to your own bedroom, and paint animals of all shapes and sizes around the top half of the walls (right).

Practical considerations at this stage revolve around safety: for your own sake, check the height of the changing table, and ensure that you have easy access to nappies (diapers) and clean clothing as you cannot leave a baby at a height to go off in search of either.

Junior bedrooms

The transition from nursery to first real bedroom and from cot (crib) to proper bed is an important step for both child and parent. Until the young child becomes accustomed to sleeping in a bed, it is wise to restrict its height off the ground to the minimum, in case the child should fall out.

If your child is hugely excited by the change of sleeping arrangements, harness that energy and try to ascertain what they want in their first bedroom. The demands may be extraordinary, prompted by peer pressure at school in the main, but listen and adapt to make it a happy room.

Young children tend to be very sociable. Nowadays, as more mothers return to work, more children than ever before will be obliged to socialize with school friends on a regular and frequent basis. If the child-minding parents are without a garden, a decent-sized child's bedroom seems the only escape from chaos. Although children take up less space than adults, if the bedroom is to become meeting-place as well as playroom and bedroom, it will either need to be bigger than you planned, or you will have to employ space-saving devices to exploit the space available.

To this end, manufacturers are designing more and more themed and modular beds. Simple bunk beds are no longer enough. Today they have to be incorporated into complicated units of shelves, drawers, tables or drawing surfaces, with special slots for computer screens and television sets. The bed units themselves tend to have built-in drawers constructed with the child's strength and size in mind, for not only are they within easy reach for someone of restricted height, but access to the drawers is simple. These will provide ample storage for anything from train sets and tin soldiers to furry animals.

Super-trendy is usually super-expensive, however, and a child's desire to keep up with his or her peers can be very oppressive and disheartening for the average parent. If your child is to have a more traditional style of bedroom, you can take infinite care over its decoration instead which will go some way to mending the situation. And involving your child as much as possible in any of the decisions that have to be made, whether concerning the size, shape and colour of the bed, or deferring to them when it comes to choosing the bed linen, will produce a rewardingly positive response. You will be well advised to avoid sheets and blankets because making beds properly is relatively difficult and time-consuming, while persuading a child to tidy a duvet each morning should be comparatively easy.

Keep an inflatable mattress on hand for unexpected overnighters; it can be stored with a duvet and pillow in a wicker basket or blanket box in a corner of the bedroom, or at the foot of the bed. If you have enough space, you might consider having a second bed in the room. It could stand against a wall as more of a day bed, used predominantly to house the overflow of soft toys from the main bed.

You can magnify the sense of excitement and adventure that a child will feel when a friend stays the night by adding some apparently spontaneous decorating touches. When the extra bed materializes, you could make up both beds to match: both with tartan blankets, or with duvets featuring opposing cartoon characters like Tom and Jerry. You could even drape sheets around the room to resemble tents or teepees, replacing the sheets on the beds with sleeping bags. You could stick silver glitter or tiny stars onto a dark ceiling to further the camping image, even hang up a mobile of a large yellow moon.

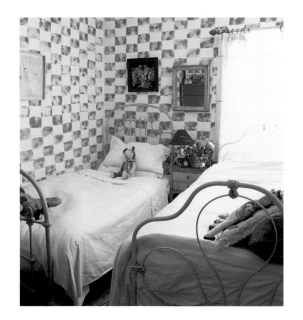

A CHILD'S CHOICE

The modular style of bedroom (opposite page) can combine every little girl's fantasy of living in her own doll's house with a clever storage idea. Each unit here is designed to resemble a house – complete with pitched roof. Easily accessible drawers with large finger holes can be approached from either side of the unit and the three units together create an effective screen for the bunk beds. The house at the head of the beds contains a bedside lamp, while the unit furthest away is equipped with a black-board and drawers for chalk and dusters.

The decoration and furnishings in both the bedrooms (left) appear simple and traditional, but both contain clever, more contemporary features. A simple, low, pine bed in a sparsely furnished room (above) has a system of wicker baskets underneath as inventive storage, making the most of the little space there is. The sponged red-and-white check paint effect (below) is ideal in a room dominated by iron-framed beds; busy, bright and cheerful, it lifts any austerity in the atmosphere. At the same time, the friendly sponged finish helps to ease the child's tastes towards the more formal designs of adult fabrics and papers.

KING OF THE CASTLE

Teenagers are always demanding so there is no reason to suppose that decorating a teenager's bedroom will be easy. The room must take on its more serious role as a study at this stage so you will also need to establish what that will require in terms of space and storage. Tidiness will be increasingly important as the child continues to grow in a finite space. If you are lucky enough to have high ceilings, you can save floor space by employing a scaffolding structure (right) with a bed platform on top. Bolted to the wall for safety, this is an imaginative, hard-working piece of furniture with a bookshelf as one end of the bed support and the access ladder as the other. The desk is positioned directly below the sleeping platform, resting on wooden trestles and supported by the central filing cabinet. An extra shelf at the side of the bed stores books and an alarm clock, as well as preventing the occupant from rolling out of bed.

As they require minimal care, duvets are perfect for a teenage bedroom, and particularly here, where bed-making is difficult and untucked sheets and blankets would spoil the structure's line.

Life in a teenage bedroom

Most teenagers will have very strong ideas of what they want and how it should be arranged, so it may be difficult to have things exactly as you want them. Remember how important that private space will be for a developing adolescent; how vital it feels to have some freedom to create your own environment; how stamping your own personality on your room is crucial to your general self-confidence and to the development of your self-image during those confusing years. It is at this age when the bedroom doubles as a study, but also where those intimate conversations with best friends over the first adolescent agonies take place.

Requirements can far exceed the size and suitability of the bedroom, with every conceivable inch of wall space taken up with magazine cuttings, postcards and pin-ups of

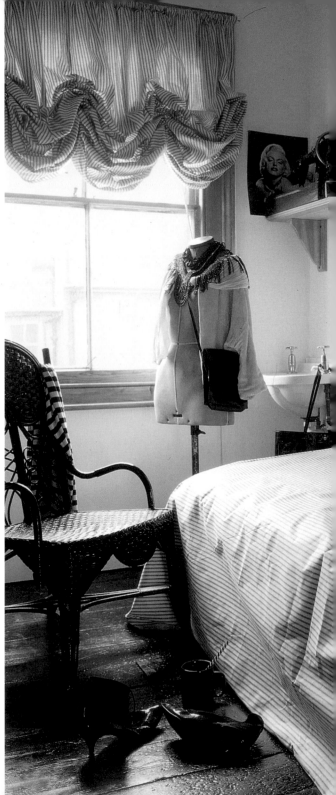

favourite idols. Overladen shelves will inevitably stagger under the weight of the latest in hi-fi equipment and pounding speakers. Compact discs will vie for space with cassettes and paperbacks, and the floor is bound to be piled high with magazines and heaps of discarded clothing and shoes, and probably dirty coffee mugs. As every available cupboard (closet) and drawer disgorges its contents to add to the chaos, you will doubtless be told that everything has a place in this disorderly scheme of things. Manufacturers continue to market new ranges of sophisticated bedroom units, meanwhile, in an attempt to help parents and children alike bring order to this mayhem.

Some children, of course, will be keen to be involved in creating a special style for their bedrooms. The mysterious disappearance of an old rug from the corridor, or some cushions from the sofa, may be the first indications that your teenage child is developing decorating fever. Traces of lurid paint in the bathroom basin and protracted periods of time behind closed doors should probably be encouraged, at whatever cost, as signs of a developing personality.

BLACK AND WHITE

Decorating monochromatically can lend an air of style and sophistication to a teenager's bedroom (centre) – just as effective and a refreshing change from bright colours. Black-and-white mattress ticking – chic and affordable – has been used for the bed cover and festoon blind to set the scene, with black-painted floorboards and wicker chair to match. The narrow strip of coordinated braid running around the top of the otherwise plain walls is a subtle touch. Marilyn Monroe could have been joined by several other black-and-white photographs to liven up the wall.

Too often a teenager's bedroom is not large enough to accommodate a spare bed for occasional overnight guests. Bunk beds may be the easy answer but they will probably be deemed juvenile; there are modular beds on the market, however, which have adapted the idea of storing a small trestle bed under a standard one, and these will solve your problem. The version illustrated here (left) comprises a base and simple mattress, forming a more than serviceable bed; it can be pulled out into the centre of the room on demand – probably by the children themselves.

INDEX

PUBLISHER'S ACKNOWLEDGMENTS

Conran Octopus would like to thank the following photographers and organizations for their permission to reproduce the photographs in this book:

1 Jean-Francois Jaussaud; 2 Paul Ryan (designer: Myra Frost)/ International Interiors; 3 David Parmiter; 4-5 Deidi von Schaewen (interior designer: Françoise Dorget); 6-7 John Hall; 7 Heiner Orten/Jalag/Sabine Oppenlander Associates; 9 Fritz von der Schulenburg (Architect:Nico Rensch)/The Interior Archive; 10 Ingalill Snitt; 11 Pascal Chevallier/Agence Top; 12-13 Jerome Darblay; 14 Nicolas Tosi (stylists:Julie Borgeaud & Anne-Marie Comte)/Marie Claire Maison; 15 Tim Street-Porter (architect: Jeffrey Tohl); 16 Peter Cook (architect: Sergison Bates)/Archipress; 17 Peter Cook (architect: Sergison Bates); 18 left Henry Bourne/Elle Decoration; 19 William Waldron; 20 left Stephane Couturier (architect: Nouvel)/Archipress; 20 right Hotze Eisma; 21 Christophe Dugied (stylist: Catherine Ardouin)/Marie Claire Maison; 22 Stephane Couturier (architect: Colomb)/Archipress; 23 Pascal Chevallier/ Agence Top; 24-5 Ingalill Snitt; 25 Jean-Pierre Godeaut; 26 David Parmiter/Homes and Gardens/Robert Harding Picture Library; 27 Ianthe Ruthven; 28-9 René Stoltie/The World of Interiors; 30 Jerome Darblay; 31 Eric Morin; 32 Tim Beddow (Architect: John Pawson) /The Interior Archive; 33 Richard Waite; 34-5 Tim Beddow (designer: Ricciardi)/The Interior Archive ; 36-7 Fritz von der Schulenberg (designer: Mimmi O'Connell)/The Interior Archive; 37 Simon McBride; 38 Hotze Eisma/V.T. Wonen; 39 Guy Bouchet/ Stock Image Production; 40 Ingalill Snitt (Stylist: Daniel Rozensztroch)/Marie Claire Maison; 41 Christian Sarramon; 42 Paul Ryan (designer:Marla Weinhoff)/International Interiors; 43 James Mortimer/The World of Interiors; 44 Hotze Eisma; 45 Mark Luscombe-Whyte/Elizabeth Whiting & Associates; 46 Jerome Darblay; 47 Henry Wilson/The Interior Archive; 48 Hotze Eisma; 49 above James Mortimer (designer: Wendy Harrop)/The Interior Archive ; 49 below Marie Pierre Morel (stylist: M. Kalt)/Marie Claire Maison; 50 Polly Wreford/Woman & Home/Robert Harding Picture Library; 51 left Chris Drake/Homes & Gardens/Robert Harding Picture Library; 52 Christian Sarramon; 53 James Merrell/Homes and Garden/Robert Harding Picture Library; 54 Tim Beddow/The Interior Archive; 55 Trevor Richards/Abode; 56-7 Fritz von der Schulenberg (Mimmi O'Connell)The Interior Archive; 57 Christian Sarramon; 58 Gilles de Chabeneix/Designers Guild bed and bedlinen, Kings Road, London; 58-9 Fritz von der Schulenberg (Adelheid von der Schulenburg)/The Interior Archive; 60 Hotze Eisma/V.T. Wonen; 61 Thomas Piek; 62 Marie Pierre Morel (le Signe & Puech)/Marie Claire Maison; Top; 63 above Pascal Chevallier/ Agence Top; 63 below Nicolas Millet/Agence; 64 Simon McBride; 65 Marie-Pierre Morel (stylist:Marion Bayle)/Marie Claire Maison; 66 Nadia Mackenzie; 67 John Hall; 68-9 Wayne Vincent (designer: Lesley Saddington)/The Interior Archive; 69 Schöner Wohnen/ Camera Press; 70-1 Jean-Francois Jaussaud; 72 left Scott Frances/ Esto; 72 right Hotze Eisma/V.T. Wonen; 73 Jan Baldwin/Domain; 74 Schöner Wohnen /Camera Press; 75 above John Hay/Voque Living; 75 below David Brittain/Domain; 76 left Jean-Paul Bonhommet/ Elizabeth Whiting & Associates 76-77 Tom Leighton/ Elizabeth Whiting & Associates.

AUTHOR'S ACKNOWLEDGMENTS

I would like to thank the professional team at Conran Octopus for their help and moral support in putting this book together. To Clare Limpus and Ruth Prentice, to Sarah Sears for showing me a glimpse of the diplomacy of editing, and to Denny Hemming for keeping me on the straight and narrow.

A final thank you to my team of stickers in the office, to Pooks, Zoe, Nancy, Sophie and Fred, for their laid back attitude in moments of crisis.